TOP TEN
WORST JOBS
IN HISTORY

by **Rob Alcraft**

illustrated by **Igor Sinkovec**

Small bendy
person wanted for
important work.

Apply here.

OXFORD
UNIVERSITY PRESS
AUSTRALIA & NEW ZEALAND

OXFORD
UNIVERSITY PRESS

Oxford University Press is a department of the University of Oxford.
It furthers the University's objective of excellence in research,
scholarship, and education by publishing worldwide. Oxford is a registered
trademark of Oxford University Press in the UK and in certain other countries.

Published in Australia by
Oxford University Press
Level 8, 737 Bourke Street, Docklands, Victoria 3008, Australia

Text © Rob Alcraft 2014, 2019

The moral rights of the author have been asserted

First published 2014
This edition 2019
Reprinted 2020, 2021

ISBN 9780190318413

Series Editor: Nikki Gamble
Designed by Oxford University Press in collaboration with Fiona Lee, Pounce Creative
Illustrated by Igor Sinkovec
Printed in Singapore by Markono Print Media Pte Ltd
Links to third party websites are provided by Oxford in good faith and for information only.
Oxford disclaims any responsibility for the materials contained in any third party website referenced in this work.

Acknowledgements

The publishers would like to thank the following for the permission to reproduce photographs:
Background images by Vector illustration/Shutterstock; Kirillov Alexey/Shutterstock.

We have made every effort to trace and contact all copyright holders before publication.
If notified, the publisher will rectify any errors or omissions at the earliest opportunity.

In the past, children as young as seven had to do awful jobs that adults didn't want to do. You young bendy people wouldn't have been lounging around – you would have been hard at work!

So, come on! Let's look back in history and see which job *you* think is the worst.

Contents

Scarecrow

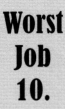

OK, easiest job first. **It's 1856.**
There are all kinds of jobs on farms for
young people like you. You can start this
one when you're just five or six years old.
You're a scarecrow!

It's your job to scare birds away from
eating seeds and plants in the fields.
You'll shout loudly – and clap bits
of wood together, too. Clack, clack!
Now do this for 12 hours, every day.

Your pay is almost nothing. But
if you're lucky, you might also
get a turnip! That's a hard,
round vegetable that's mostly
fed to farm animals. Now
there's something to look
forward to! Come on,
clack, clack!

The hours are long and the pay is terrible, but this job is easy compared to some!

The horrible truth

George Edwards started working as a scarecrow when he was six. He got so tired and bored that he fell asleep. The farmer fined him two days' wages!

Tanner's Apprentice

It's 1347. Tanners make leather from animal skins. As the **apprentice**, you're a tanner's live-in helper. You have to do all the nasty stuff.

First, you scrape the animal skin to clean it. Then you have to wash the skin. Tubs of old **urine** are good for getting off all that dead animal hair. That's right, dunk it in the urine!

Next, the skin needs to be softened in a thick soup of water and dog waste. The skins need a proper squeeze, so they go in a tub — and you do, too! Stamp your feet. Get those toes working!

6

There's no pay for this job, and you can't leave until your training is over. Also, you stink! But at least you make leather!

Truly horrid

Bearable

Horrible

Oh-no-o-meter

The horrible truth

Apprentices had almost no control over what happened to them. In 1347, a young apprentice tanner called Ellis was given away to a new master. He had no say in it at all.

7

Pickpocket

It's 1833. What do you do if you can't get a proper job? Crime is your only choice.

Criminal gangs love an enthusiastic small person like you. Pickpocketing is a common job – you even get training! You work with other young thieves, stealing things from pockets, bags and shops. It's simple: grab whatever you can, then run!

Just don't get caught. You can be locked up in jail for months, or even **executed**, just for stealing an apple or a pair of shoes. You could even be **transported** to another country. You might never come back!

If you can steal, you won't starve. But if you get caught, the punishments are harsh.

Bearable Horrible Truly horrid

Oh-no-o-meter

The horrible truth

In 1833, nine-year-old Nicholas White was caught stealing some paint. He was sentenced to death, but was transported to Australia instead.

Gong Farmer's Child

It's 1536. Gong farmers clean out toilets, and they need small people like you to help them. But these aren't the kind of toilets that flush ...

The waste from toilets goes into a pit. Someone has to clean out the pit so it doesn't overflow. That person is you!

You work at night because nobody wants to see you or smell you. You fit perfectly into the small spaces of the awful pit — where adults don't want to go. The gong farmer needs someone your size to squeeze up the narrow drains and give them a good scrape.

Sure, you'll be wading around in human filth, but at least you'll be well paid.

In you go!

The flip side

Gong farmers cleaned out Queen Elizabeth I's royal toilets at Hampton Court Palace. It was a horrible job, but they were paid well. And they could sell the waste afterwards, for **fertiliser**!

Maid Servant

It's 1880. Servants are very common. Some very rich families have a whole team of servants. But many people only have a maid. You're still a servant, but you're on your own. As a maid, you do all the things that nobody else wants to do.

You probably sleep in the kitchen, or in a cupboard. It doesn't really matter – you don't lie down much.

You start first thing in the morning by collecting and emptying the potties. Then you move on to cleaning fireplaces and stoves, sweeping, laying tables, cooking and cleaning.

Scrub, scrub! You can fit in two or three hours of work before breakfast. Then there's laundry, fetching, carrying, cooking, polishing, sweeping ... it's endless!

Oh-no-o-meter

Bearable • Horrible • Truly horrid

You're all alone, and the jobs are tiring – and never-ending.

The horrible truth

Laundry maids in one large house had 600 items to sort, scrub, wash, dry, **starch** and iron every week. That's one item every ten minutes!

Powder Monkey

It's 1759. A powder monkey is a young, bendy person like you who lives on a warship. Your job is to carry tubs of gunpowder to the cannons. Powder monkeys are supposed to be at least 12 years old, but they're often younger.

It's a dangerous job, but quite simple. Your warship sails close to enemy warships, and then the blasting begins. *Fire!*

Cannonballs and bits of metal smash through the warship. Deadly, razor-sharp splinters of wood explode from the **hull**. But you ignore the deafening, smoky chaos. You have to run! Go to the store room, collect another tub of gunpowder, then get back to your cannon. Ready? *Go!*

It's a hard life at sea, and the danger is extreme – and terrifying.

BOOM!

The flip side

A boy called Equiano (*say* eh-kwi-ar-no) fought as a powder monkey on the English warship *Namur* in 1759. There were many other young boys working on the ship, so an on-board school was created, where Equiano was educated.

Mill Scavenger

It's 1799. Cotton mills are **factories** where dangerous machines spin thread to make cloth. While the machines whir away, you have to squeeze underneath them to pick up fluff and broken threads.

Be careful not to leave any of your body parts behind! They can easily get trapped in all the fast-moving metal and wood. Concentrate!

Pay, by the way, is around 17 pence per week. That will buy a bit of bread. You work 14 hours or more each day. But don't worry — if you get tired, you'll be dunked upside down in a tub of cold water. That should wake you up!

You're paid pennies and you work crazy hours. You suffer regular punishment and risk injury every day.

The horrible truth

In 1799, Robert Blincoe started work as a scavenger in a cotton mill. He was just seven years old. Apart from having heavy weights hung from his ears as punishment, he was lucky – he only lost half a finger.

Coal Putter

It's 1842. As a coal putter, your job is to help get coal out of a mine. You can start work when you're around seven or eight years old.

You work deep underground, pushing and pulling heavy trolleys full of coal for 12 hours or more each day. You crawl through dark tunnels full of water, and get bald patches from pushing the trolleys with your head.

It's awful, but you small people are the only ones who can do this. The tunnels are no higher than your waist. Adults and horses won't fit. So, off you go. Giddy up!

You work hard for very little money, with the risk of rock-falls and mine-gas explosions.

When I grow up, I want to be a horse.

The horrible truth

Mary Hague started work as a coal putter at age nine. In 1842, a mines inspector asked her if she liked her job. Guess what? She didn't!

Roman Slave

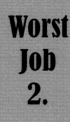

It's the year 53. As a slave in ancient Rome, you do *all* the work. You're good value, too — you cost about the same as a small horse.

But don't worry, some of your jobs aren't so bad. You might be put to work cleaning your owner's skin. Or perhaps you might have to pluck out their armpit hair! You could even be a doorman, chained to the door so you can't wander off.

If you try to run away, things can get very nasty. You'll have "FUG" — short for the Roman word for runaway — burned into your forehead. Then you'll be worked to death in the mines. Better get back to plucking that armpit hair!

The only good thing about this job is that there may be a chance to buy your freedom. Better start saving!

Oh-no-o-meter

Bearable Horrible Truly horrid

The flip side

Dionysius (*say* Die-on-iss-ee-us) was a Roman slave who ran away from his master. He was never caught. Dionysius was last seen 200 miles away, and still running!

Sweep

It's 1819. People burn coal for heat and cooking. There are chimneys everywhere. As a sweep, your job is to clean the chimneys — by climbing up inside them! You can start work at around age six — the smaller you are, the better.

There's poisonous **soot** to scrape and brush. Some of the chimneys you squeeze through are no wider than the open book you're holding now.

Not keen? It doesn't matter. If you're a smallish **orphan** with no home, you can be bought for a very cheap price, and simply put to work. Up you go!

Right, which job do you want? Time to choose!

You can suffocate, be burned or just get stuck. What's more, the soot will give you horrible diseases!

Well, come on! It's not going to sweep itself!

The horrible truth

In 1819, the chimneys at England's Windsor Castle were climbed and cleaned by two little sweep sisters. And who was their master? Their dad!

Glossary

apprentice: someone learning how to do a job

executed: sentenced to death

factories: places where things are made

fertiliser: something added to farm land to help crops grow

hull: the outside surface of a ship

orphan: a child whose mother and father are no longer living

soot: the black powder left by smoke in a chimney

starch: spray clothes to make them stiff

transported: shipped to another country as a kind of slave

urine: the yellow liquid that takes waste out of the body

Index